I0078910

# THE CONSOLATION OF GEOMETRY

## ALICE CAMPBELL ROMANO
### POEMS

**C&R Press**
Conscious & Responsible

All Rights Reserved.

Printed in the United States of America

First Edition
1 2 3 4 5 6 7 8 9

Selections of up to two pages may be reproduced without permission. To reproduce more than two pages of any one portion of this book, write to C&R Press publishers John Gosslee and Andrew Ibis.

Copyright ©2024 Alice Campbell Romano
ISBN 978-1-949540-56-7

C&R Press
Conscious & Responsible
crpress.org

For special discounted bulk purchases, please contact: sales@crpress.org

# THE CONSOLATION
# OF GEOMETRY

# TABLE OF CONTENTS

Birdsong Long Before I Was Born                                      9

Every Decade, The Cells of the Skeleton Replace Themselves   10

The Armature on Which Their Flesh Is Formed                  12

The First Time You Spoke to Me                               13

And So                                                       14

We Married in an Open Field a Wide                           15

What We Throw Away                                           16

Mists                                                        18

In Those Days                                                19

Oh, Look at That Beautiful Family                            20

This Is a Man Who Gets Things Done                           21

May We Spend Our Years as a Tale That Is Told                22

The Reef                                                     23

A Name Can Be Used as a Bludgeon                             24
    and Inflict Invisible Bruises

In Every Marriage There Will Be Quantum Suicide              26

The New World Explorer Is Gaffed                             27

Properties of Acids                                          28

Spiderwebs in the Back Yard, 5:00 A.M                        29

Those Exploring a Reef Environment                           30

The Wound                                                    31

Long Ago When We Had Children—                               33

St. Mommy of the Improper Response                           34

Why I Stayed                                    36

In My Unbelief                                  38

Turn of the Century                             40

And So                                          41

Word of the Day                                 42

Her Husband                                     43

Every Morning, He Sits in His Chair to Dress    44

His Turn to Take Care of Me                     45

On the Terrace There Is a Chill                 46

Morning Song                                    47

Small Secrets                                   48

The Consolation of Geometry                     49


Notes                                           52
Acknowledgements                                53
About the Author                                54

# BIRDSONG LONG BEFORE I WAS BORN

Outside my room the virago stakes her claim,
her shrieks like red streaks on mothballed ships
rotting over decades in the harbor at Nanking

where I have never been—but here I am, poised on the
cliff, disguised as an impossible hummingbird, beak deep
in a red hibiscus bloom, to sip the screams of men about

to be beheaded, women raped, babies dashed on rocks,
just some more horrors of war and not even our war,
though a case may be made that all wars are the wars

of all of us. And on she rants, heaping her displeasure
on my drunken father whose retorts sound as pale thunder:
far-off bombs that pound factories and spew collateral

of kitchen sinks and baby blankets. I can't close my ears.
Neuroscientists put babies into scanners now, see tender
gray matter ignite as actors shout furious nonsense.

The more conflict at home, the sharper baby brains light up.
No wonder we love war. We connect to the people we love,
even to their wrath, with our own angry noise.

# EVERY DECADE, THE CELLS OF THE SKELETON REPLACE THEMSELVES

I heard it on television
    the night you killed yourself at the Rome Hilton.

Your friend told me
    when I left you,
        you smashed
            our Sardinian
    dinnerware
against the apartment walls,
    plate-by-plate
every piece
    shattered
        to red smithereens.

After years, I imagined the hotel bathroom.
    The mottled Carrara
        the tentative cut

        the second,
        final
        cut.

The straight razor. Honed.

                ALICE CAMPBELL ROMANO

What it took for you to lift it,
to engage your own amber eyes

your amber eyes

The firm last cut.
Blood.

.     Not about me,
          suicidologists insist.

Still I know you cursed me
          when you sketched
          the first
      thin, red line. Took courage
        for the next cut.

Your curse — a mist of tiny needles,
a sharp rain, always in my face.

# THE ARMATURE ON WHICH THEIR
## FLESH IS FORMED

Some men have at their core a magnet of desire
charged by a constant current of electric need.


Heat smolders outward, as from a night-banked fire
through skin, drawing women to them.


And men. I feel the pull in the easy way they stand,
before they turn and catch my gaze. Such men


use the power behind their eyes to start a blaze.
I am wary. I look away, deny the draw,


but weak as crumbled leaves,
I burn.

# THE FIRST TIME YOU SPOKE TO ME

You said, in English,

*In my culture,*
*we don't believe*
*in divorce.*

You raised your glass
down the long table

littered with torn shells—
*langostine, gamberetti—*

the parchment table-cover
a blood-flecked license

to accept what is presented
at the feast.

Lunch was over.
Busboys hovered like gulls.

You sucked the juice
out of me

with your blue eyes.

# AND SO

we begin again

you said

after each of us had left another belly-up in the gutter

we began again

all right

ALICE CAMPBELL ROMANO

## WE MARRIED IN AN OPEN FIELD A WIDE

and rolling plain of yellow wheat
    that fell away and away in a burn
        of light, far into decades not yet sown.

We married into the instant of
    sunlight on your flushed cheek.
        We married, and paid scant attention

to the hills, clasped as we were
    in our own brown furrow.
        We married. And, as the years

spun away, what we reaped was
    sometimes chaff, blind as we were
        to seeds of discord in the burn.

# WHAT WE THROW AWAY

A long time ago, such a long time ago,
in Greece, certainly it was Greece,
we had no place to sleep,
our friends' boat was late to dock
and we spent the night sweating on a bed
in a blue room above a bar, hot, oh God,
the air was hot and loud, and we were
too sweaty to want sex, but we did it
anyway, we were that young, and we
slipped on each other's limbs, that's how
sweaty wet we were, but we laughed
and licked the sheen from each other's
necks and knew the planet was much
too hot if this is what a summer night
was like in an island village of stucco
painted white to deflect the sun by day,
aligned to catch the water breeze by night
and the cool hill clouds, but we forgot our
revelation and got up the next morning
and found our friends and sailed around
the point to dive for amphorae, planted
for the tourists, maybe, or I'd rather think
dumped as trash two thousand years

ALICE CAMPBELL ROMANO

ago, such benign trash, terra cotta with
tiny fish flickering in and out in schools,
and I don't believe we thought about
trash as it soon would be, plastic and
ubiquitous, and ruinous, but of course
we kept our own rubbish on board, of
course we did, and we dove and stayed
cool and loved each other, and it was
all such a long time ago.

# MISTS

I love a steam room for its pewter reflections, shapes
of seated ghosts all but invisible in silver fog, the thick
whoosh of the door when I slip into a room swollen
with pale, wet heat, white as a winter day, only to find

that I've slid through time and space into a cold car
on the *autostrada* near Milan half a century ago together
with the man of my reckless desire. We can see nothing
outside the car but *nebbia,* solid cloud, not even another

car. He drives by unceasing increments, through a wall
that never opens, pallor that absorbs the world beyond
our front seat—where I watch his hands, rigid on the wheel.
*No place to go but forward,* he says. *We won't hit anyone.*

I wish I'd been afraid. But I was blind. So much hidden
in the mist would be struck so hard, revealed unbidden.

ALICE CAMPBELL ROMANO

# IN THOSE DAYS

You had a hard, hasty way
that rose with the earliest
streak of sunlight.

You shifted closer,
spooned me, touched me awake:
breasts, belly, hip.

I slept at the rim of our wide bed,
in a tight ball like a cave dog.
You cajoled me

out of untamed dreams.
The first thrusts of your strong day
shaped me to you.

# OH, LOOK AT THAT BEAUTIFUL FAMILY

We arrived with 11 suitcases and two little boys
in the days when the people who were to pick
people up at the airport stood in a gallery above
Customs, scanned the swarming floor for their
families. My mother and my aunt watched for us.
Oh—look at that beautiful family, my mother told
me she'd said in the instant before she recognized
the beautiful family as us.

Husband, young and vulnerable and hiding each
well, has taken charge of passports and luggage.
He swings suitcases up onto the counter where
an official pats and prods while I stand by and hold
close the boys and let their daddy shepherd us into
the new life he chose.

ALICE CAMPBELL ROMANO

## THIS IS A MAN WHO GETS THINGS DONE

He pulls on confidence like a diver's wetsuit.
Even to the speed fins on feet and hands.
He's been tapped to open A New York Office.
I'd have stayed in Italy, my chosen home, but
he knows he's right. He will part the unfamiliar
waters of America by his will, everything under
complete control.

# MAY WE SPEND OUR YEARS AS A TALE THAT IS TOLD
*Thou turnest man back to the dust. Psalm 90*

Old men who, by reason of strength,
      live to eighty or more,
will bend forward when they walk,
      and roll their shoulders in

so that their arms droop
      and the palms of their hands,
the frail, faded palms of the elderly,
      face backwards and quaver.

My husband, my strength, when you
      are old, will you
brush back secret sins with tiny
      tremors of regret?

While we two are fierce, keep tight
      my hands in yours, and I will
hold hard to you, so when it is our time
      to turn back to dust,

the young will say of us that we loved
      our days, that we
rejoiced and were glad and made no
      shame to scatter in our wake.

ALICE CAMPBELL ROMANO

# THE REEF

His ambitions invent themselves, burst forth from
the sand, are never mirages, always attainable. Each
a new Atlantis. He discounts fierce coral on the
way. Jagged barriers that sting worst are subtle,
cultural, defy explanation. American humor eludes
him. He barely laughs. He reads books in English to
advance what he knows, never to escape. He travels
to film markets around the globe, brings home the
bacon, the fatted cow, the fruits of his labor, and
misses the holidays. He parlays shabby two-story
buildings into town squares, bends bankers to his
vision, his wife to his needs. When he is away, I
keep his chair open at the top of the table. He is a
stranger to his children.

*If a diver runs into a piece of coral and receives a*
*scrape or abrasion, the soft covering of the coral is*
*torn off the rough lower layer and deposited into*
*the created wound. This leads to prolonged healing*
*time, with some coral scrapes taking months—*
*no, decades—to heal.*

## A NAME CAN BE USED AS A BLUDGEON
## AND INFLICT INVISIBLE BRUISES


I saw a stranger clubbed
by the side of the road,
balled up like a pill bug
to save his skull from


an aggressor gone berserk.
I need, merely, to flinch from
my name, slim syllables
you breathed once in soft


seduction, not this cudgel
of frustration you swing
to enforce your complaints,
a name swollen in wrath.


What if—instead—you
were to flourish a thin switch
of my delicate name in a
game of dashing linguistic


elan—could I then parry
your lashings, make you
dance for each slice you
might flick from my heart?


Alice Campbell Romano

No. As the assailant
by the side of the road seeks
in his shoulder the shudder,
the thunk, of each blow,

you need for your rage
to shiver then wane
along the bludgeon
you've made of my name.

# IN EVERY MARRIAGE
## THERE WILL BE QUANTUM SUICIDE

If I shoot myself on this patio, the theory goes, I survive
in Many-Worlds. Each path doesn't simply quit
after it bends at the yellow undergrowth.

I stomped, I cried, I threw things. I screamed at Mother.
Husband—did I choose you as my lover or my penance?
Many-Worlds: Where Mother doesn't always bare her

teeth behind her bright red lips and Daddy doesn't drive away
to the bars. Husband—you can't know I'm not alive, or dead.
Or alive and dead. Some days, you'll like me dead. Others,

as long as I compose your emails, cook your food, stifle my
retorts, you're satisfied. Husband, of course you have *your*
lives too. Innumerable—don't you just *adore* it!—infinite

permutations of *you*. But may the god of quantum mechanics
grant me this: that in some—at least some—of all the parallel,
all the Many-Worlds, I will never, no, *never* run into you.

# THE NEW WORLD EXPLORER IS GAFFED

*Gaff. (a): something painful or difficult to bear; ordeal; especially: persistent raillery or criticism. (b): rough treatment, abuse.*
*Merriam-Webster Dictionary*

Don't watch the giant sea bass
on its back, in the open air,

on a hard deck. It smashes
the deck, gasps, curls, twists,

leaps—on the unforgiving
surface of this unexpected life.

Fish out of water,
breakdance artist.

No one is allowed
to know his struggle

for oxygen, for
the lost air of home.

PROPERTIES OF ACIDS
*Fractions of acid in follicular fluid at conception*
*increase chances of a female child.*

He tells me
when he's on a rant
every three months or so

*You're a miserable, unhappy woman,*
*negative even before I finish my sentence.*
*You can't change. It's in your cells.*

I have to wonder: is it?
I am female. And when
he rages at me because I dare

to speak, he insults this woman.
Acids have the ability to conduct
electricity. The air crackles,

we both are shocked. Acids etch
metal surfaces in order to create designs,
and to purify. Caustic I may be,

and I'll examine that, but the base
metal he is made of is brighter, sharper,
because of the abilities of acid.

ALICE CAMPBELL ROMANO

# SPIDERWEBS IN THE BACK YARD, 5:00 A.M.

Vermillion bougainvillea drops a deep,
soft-misted swag down half the garden wall.
I've been away. Last night, I couldn't sleep.
It's barely light, and I'm outside—to call
on spiderwebs pearled in dew, to admire
the tension of spun gossamer, steel strings
racked against red bracts by diligent wives
I don't see. Swings upon purposeful swings,
they build webs to survive—and eat the mate.
I see a spider—she begins her snare,
dangles at the end of the first innate
filament, takes momentum from the air—
prepares to rise, to cast the next tense strand.
Does she know now how it can all unwind?

# THOSE EXPLORING A REEF ENVIRONMENT

*must use care to avoid touching any animals*
*in the habitat and should not hesitate to seek*
*medical attention when problems arise.*

ALICE CAMPBELL ROMANO

# THE WOUND

He minimized, played the hero, bore
unbearable pain, lied to me, lied to himself,
kidded himself—through four months of

dying flesh. Got better, against the odds.
Tribute to his strength. And to me, wife—
who changed dressings in our bedroom

at the top of the stairs—fitted out like
Florence Nightingale's field tent—up and
down the stairs, up and down the stairs—

*It's good for you,* he said, *and bring me
the newspaper when you come up again.*
Florence does it all, peels the dressing off

the leg two times a day, measures the gash
that gets no smaller, notes darker purple skin,
drives the patient to the City, to the surgeon

he doesn't like, and back again. And again.
And again. What do I remember from
the summer that never was? The smell.

We found a wound specialist, a fat, funny man,
genial, who tells it like it is. *I don't want to
say this,* he said, when my husband would not

comply, walked against orders and lied about
how much, *but there's a chance*, he said, *I mean,*
*we're not there yet, but if this doesn't get better,*

*he could lose his leg.* He wouldn't tell me what
it's supposed to smell like, so I said, *Dirty feet,*
*with a hint of decomposition? Yeah,* the wound

guy said, *that's about right. That's what we have,*
*so tell him to stay off it.* I did, he wouldn't. But,
with an introduction from someone he admired,

my husband graduated to a number-one specialist,
a well-known university specialist, someone
people listen to, and at last the edges knit.

And he does walk again. And our summer that
never was wrapped the book I didn't finish and
the poems I never wrote in a stench I won't forget.

ALICE CAMPBELL ROMANO

LONG AGO WHEN WE HAD CHILDREN—

little children—and they had hung
their stockings, we stayed awake downstairs
until Santa's hot chocolate grew cold

and our wine was dregs. We wrapped whatever
hadn't yet been wrapped, trucks and the like,
with many edges that could not logically

be wrapped, but we wrapped. We unrolled
brittle wrapping paper from the dollar store
in garish reds and greens. We never enjoyed

the help of a good pair of scissors. One of us
had always abused the lean desk shears one
of us had bought, pressed them into service

on gristly garden hoses. When we thought
we had enough paper for the truck or the
action figure, you would hold a yardstick

firm along the roll edge of the Christmas paper,
and I would tear that cheap paper ragged,
and we'd reach for the wine and the scotch tape.

and that night I would dream of a bright
brigade of scissors at my service,
and perfection under the tree.

# ST. MOMMY OF THE IMPROPER RESPONSE

I didn't call the cops,
when you whipped the boys
with insults, when you parted the air

ahead of you like a bullet to charge
for me, your wife, the one person who
could hold your blame; when you

closed a door in cool deliberation
so you could, unseen, drive a fist
into my side and still advance

until I fell back on the floor, arms up
so as to keep your feet from my face—
but you would not have struck my face—

you never did, except by mistake,
because people would see and
suspect, but you kicked when I

was down: my hips, my back, my arms,
while I curled on the floor and you
cursed me for my failure. I didn't

speak up, over and over and over and over
and again, shuttered in silence from public
shame. I accepted the tendered gold ring,

the string of pearls, the fine leather handbag,
the silk stole so thick it rolled from hand to
hand in waves. I took the presents for amends

I believed you couldn't say in words.
There was always a next time when you
needed me to fault, until at last I had no self,

so when the littlest boy came down the hall,
jelly toast crumbs at the corner of his mouth,
ready for me to drive him to school

with his brother who stayed in the kitchen,
crunching toast to cover his daddy's yelling,
I said, Everything's fine, Sweetie. Just fine.

WHY I STAYED

There was the day when no one but you
and I were home, fighting, until time for
me to pick up the boys from school, but

instead, I picked up the letter opener
and jammed it in my gut. Not deep enough.
I slammed a gauze pad on the wound and

some tape and you watched and said
I was crazy and of course I was, because
if I'd been sane, I'd have picked up the boys

and never come back. But we led a charming
life. Beautiful family, business built from your
energy, my American education. Besides,

my mother would have said *I warned you.*
She was always right. Her jibes with knife
lips and tossed head about your vision of how

she should make money from her land—*Build
two houses here,* you insisted. *And tennis courts*
where soared ancient oaks—she balanced by

summers for the children by the Hudson,
evenings of fireflies, tenderness without shouts.
The last time I failed at marriage I carry

with me every day, a prickling in the skin.
I must not fail again, not for me, not for
the gold, not even to sidestep shame,

but because I see you, traveling father, diver
into the treacherous bliss, fish out of water,
so raw, so naked, your skin soft like a boy's,

your blue eyes that beg me to value what you
bring to our feast, your young face turned to
mine, as vulnerable as the day we landed here.

# IN MY UNBELIEF

*If you want to see Rob alive, come now.*
    Four-thirty in the morning. Our younger boy
        calls us to his brother's side. Coats over

        sleepwear, L.A./San Francisco first plane.
    Scared son in the hospital lobby, manly.
Big brother Rob in the O.R.. Assault.

Elderly surgeon, roused from home at dawn, expert
    in subdural hematomas, saws open our boy's skull
        to vacuum out his blood, his brain, but we

        must not think of that. And you, husband,
    have vanished into a room off the lobby to work your phone.
Your genius, to make connections, keep track

of people you meet whom you might want to
    keep, for any reason. You call them friends.
        I thought they were just people you could use.

        I focus on the brown corduroy jacket the old doctor
    wears to go home...*May not...will never...even if...*
We listen, but you, Rob's father, stiffen, nod,

seize an aide's sleeve, demand each report,
    every feeble prognostication, hands open
        over the counter to receive papers that

          ALICE CAMPBELL ROMANO

click-click from printers, papers only you
could conjure so early in the game, this mortal
game whose end you will determine,

not the defeatist surgeon who says he did his *best…*
*but we can't stop the swelling…pressure…damage…*
Rob's head, huge, on a blue pillow. Coma.

A new doctor hits the unit, up from Los Angeles.
His radical protocol to drain fluid from brains
after trauma needs more subjects. He is sure.

You, father, husband, found this brave new doctor,
groundbreaking answer to time-worn corduroy.
From your first call in the hospital lobby,

intimate in your dread, still wearing pajamas,
you worked networks of friends—yes, friends—
until you found the match for our son's need.

Weeks, months, afterward, you traveled the coast,
solved the impossible, helped us to help you, made us
believe it would all be well, and it was, it is.

Our boys were born in Italy, where they say
*a mother gives her newborn to the light.*
Dearest, you gave the light back to our son.

# TURN OF THE CENTURY

You brought your family—wife and children—
home for the new millennium. Cousins by the dozens, shoulder
to shoulder in the piazza outside the palazzo where you grew up,

where your mother lay on her bed and feared to
be left alone. The party churned outside her windows, sucked
everyone into the square to pay homage to *Due Mila*.

The d.j.—one of your nephews—spun a mix of
Italian pop that made the island bounce. Our sons were on stage
with him, but our daughter had vanished into the crowd, into

the surge of young, drunk, handsome Italian boys.
A few circled the square on tilted Vespas, girls slung behind, down
to the beach, down on the sand, down with the beat from the d.j..

In your mother's bedroom, her sons and daughters
and spouses whispered in and out, like smoke from a genie's lamp.
I came up from the piazza, into the house, and from your moth-
er's room,

I heard our daughter laugh. Then I heard your
mother laugh. Then you came up behind me and held my shoul-
ders and said, *She's our daughter. We made that girl. I love you.*

ALICE CAMPBELL ROMANO

AND SO

I will begin again

with you

this time I must not raise my voice

I will change

my side of the seesaw

move the fulcrum

make my own peace

with us

choose to love you

WORD OF THE DAY
*Forecastle:* sailors' quarters on a ship.


I know little of sailors on long voyages—
but the word *fore…castle* does have my breath


coming shorter and I hear myself whisper—
perhaps later tonight, at the kitchen counter—


*Yes, touch my forecastle, touch me, touch my breasts.*
Arouse at least the figurehead of me that leads the ship,


my image merely the most recent in the antique mirror
beside the stairs. One night this mirror will release its


captured images. Two hundred and fifty years
of men and women in silvery embroidered satin,


and other relatives in rougher, common cloth,
will stream up and down my staircase in moonlight,


unmindful of the fancy figure that for my husband
is his wife, a woman who sees, when reflection


takes the wheel, that I dry out, crack and splinter.
Siren eyes and mermaid scales no longer lead


the way. The paint already flakes.
The logbook writes itself each day.


ALICE CAMPBELL ROMANO

# HER HUSBAND

My wife comes to me in bed
shy. I like that she wants

to please me, cares what I will see,
as if I were exempt from time.

Shining from her shower, wrapped
in her robe, she says, *I hate my body.*

She remembers her flat belly,
thin waist, fine skin. But this

woman, here, now, this is my
wife, and all the years between us—

so I want to tell her *I love you,*
and I never know why that's so hard.

But I say this: *I love your body.*
*Take off the robe.*

*Don't turn out the light.*

# EVERY MORNING, HE SITS IN HIS CHAIR TO DRESS

He dangles, then shakes, his shorts
over his feet, until first one leg-opening,
then the other, is positioned so he can

prod each foot into each hole. He leans
forward to synchronize his boxers, then pulls
them up over calves muscled by recumbent

biking, past knees each with a vertical
white scar where crazy-glue closed his skin
above titanium and which never will be flexible

again, so he must perform this dangle and shake
just to pull his pants on every day, up over his
hard thighs, and then, a last tiny lift to the finish:

over the butt, up the front, to a waist no broader
than when he was forty, and now he stands.
This time, it's his slacks he shakes to the mat.

He sits, repeats, rises, almost completely dressed
for the day, another day he will pull into shape
out of habit or love.

ALICE CAMPBELL ROMANO

# HIS TURN TO TAKE CARE OF ME

before the
lockdown
before anyone
knew what we
were all in for
I was very sick
with something else,
doesn't matter what,
fever, delirium,
hospitals,
what's important
is how he gave up
all his plans so as
to stay near me,
how he
brought me home
and kept me safe
and cool and clean
and never once
complained
of what
he had lost or
of a stench.

## ON THE TERRACE, THERE IS A CHILL

You step outside and I look up.
Your sweater is exactly the blue

of the October sky behind you.
You cross your arms, draw your

sweater over your head. Your shirt is
the same blue. The sun blinds but I'm

not blinded, am I? One with heaven, you
blend into the blue of a Giotto fresco.

*Here, amore mio,* you say, *put on
my sweater. You're shivering.*

# MORNING SONG

I wake up before you, some mornings.
You sleep without a sound, quite still.

We grow old, we grow older. We grow
meager like my bones. My arms above

our blanket, parched, the fragrant oils
massaged in last night's fire-lit illusion

dissipated. I grapple for the lurking phrase,
engaged in a persistent game inside my head.

You sleep without a sound, too still.
At last, the blanket rises with your breath.

# SMALL SECRETS

I take pride in a well-set table
and a well-made bed.

The first because I have the privilege of food
which I am fortunate to share

and which tastes better when linen is fresh
and glassware shines.

The next, because when my husband
climbs the stairs after his day is over

he is old and he hurts. The broad bed,
the smooth spread, color and texture varied

according to the season, upright pillows on duty
to support our shoulders until we have read

ourselves to gape-mouthed sleep
and one of us reminds the other

to turn out the light. We pull the pillows
under our heads, slide down into sheets

both taut and soft, and reach hand to hand
to touch goodnight.

ALICE CAMPBELL ROMANO

# THE CONSOLATION OF GEOMETRY
*Inside Richard Serra*


The house tilts. Parents shriek,
storm into rooms. Any surface
becomes an unsafe thing.
The crack can never be repaired. Even now,
I can be cornered in a sharp


angle by the person who lives
with me. I cringe,
as if about to be hit. I come to myself
in a place where the floor
is torqued, unstable, tilts. I'm afraid to take


a step. I face a high, curved
wall. There is no top
to this space, this ellipse.
Light washes down the wall, shows it
to be hematite, the color of iron named for


blood. I am inside a
massive metal sculpture.
But I am also inside a heart,
a womb, a living redness. I inch to
the wall. If I can hold to the wall, shuffle along it,

I will reach an opening
where I can escape this enclosure.
Instead, I come face-to-face with
another curved, blood-metal wall. I stand
between the two walls, can know only

the two red walls and the
path between them where the floor
is flat. I step. The ground is firm.
I am in a canyon in Arizona. Ancient, sacred.
From over the outside wall, a crow

disciplines her child. The
child will do as it wants,
will pound on the wall.
The metal will vibrate with a deep
thrum and the deep thrum

will pulse through me
and the broken bits of me
will coalesce in the fullness of
the sound, and I will become whole
in the safety of a timeless place and a dark, red hum.

ALICE CAMPBELL ROMANO

# NOTES

Information about Coral Reefs is from USA Today's Coral Reefs & Injuries to People, Travel Tips, On-Line

The title, WE MARRIED IN AN OPEN FIELD AND WIDE, P. 10, is from Shane McCrae's poem, Horses Running Fast.

# ACKNOWLEDGEMENTS

Sometimes in a slightly different version, these poems have appeared in the following publications, for which the author is grateful.

BIRDSONG LONG BEFORE I WAS BORN
Prometheus Dreaming

THE ARMATURE ON WHICH THEIR FLESH IS FORMED
Writing in a Woman's Voice

IN EVERY MARRIAGE THERE WILL BE QUANTUM SUICIDE
Ninetenths2

MAY WE SPEND OUR YEARS AS A TALE THAT IS TOLD
Westwood Press

MORNING SONG
Quartet

ON THE TERRACE THERE IS A CHILL
Willows Wept

PROPERTIES OF ACIDS
Ninetenths2

SPIDERWEBS IN THE BACK YARD, 5:00 AM
The Raven Review

ST. MOMMY OF THE IMPROPER RESPONSE
Writing in a Woman's Voice

THE CONSOLATION OF GEOMETRY
Pink Panther Magazine

WHAT WE THROW AWAY
The Marbled Sigh, Issue No. 3

# ABOUT ALICE CAMPBELL ROMANO

A poem is the face of what we've lived. Everything is soaked in all that came before. Alice Campbell Romano lived 13 years in Rome, Italy, turning Italian sceneggiature into American movie scripts. She married a dashing Italian; they raised their family in Rome and in Los Angeles where Alice became President of The Independent Writers of Southern California (IWOSC) and worked with independent film and TV producers as well as for Universal Studios. Alice is a published and anthologized poet. She is an active member of The Hudson Valley Writers' Center in the Hudson Highlands where she grew up amid tall oaks that make an appearance in *The Consolation of Geometry*, her first book.

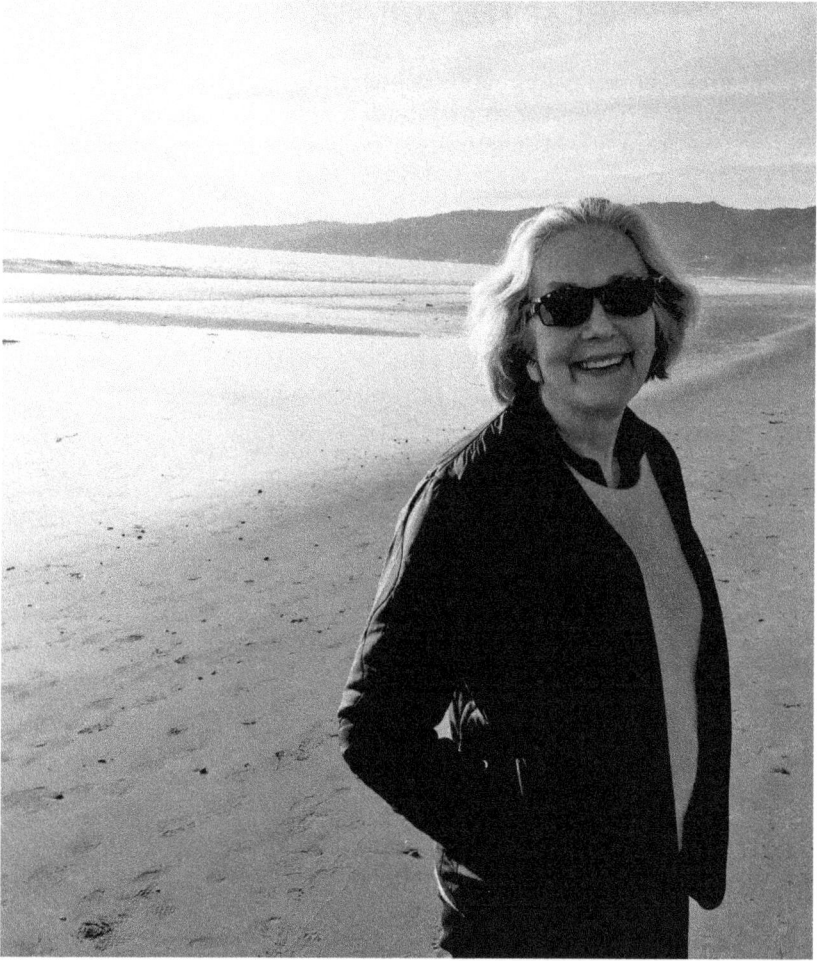

ALICE CAMPBELL ROMANO

# C&R PRESS CHAPBOOKS

C&R Press hosts two chapbook selection periods from June to September and November to March each year. The Summer Tide Pool and Winter Soup Bowl Chapbook Series are open to new and established writers in poetry, fiction, essay and other creative writing genres.

2023 SUMMER TIDE POOL
*The Consolation of Geometry* by Alice Campbell Romano

2023 WINTER SOUP BOWL
*Dinner at Las Heras* Allison A. deFreese's translation from the Spanish of Luciana Jazmín-Coronado

2022 SUMMER TIDE POOL
*The Ice Beneath the Earth* by Brian Ascalon Roley

2022 WINTER SOUP BOWL
*tommy noun* by Maurya Kerr

2021 SUMMER TIDE POOL
*Rocketflower* by Matthew Meade

2021 WINTER SOUP BOWL
*We Face the Tremenedous Meat on the Teppan* by Naoko Fujimoto

2020 WINTER SOUP BOWL
*My Roberto Clemente* by Rick Hilles

2019 SUMMER TIDE POOL
*Inside the Orb of an Oracle* by Dannie Ruth

2019 WINTER SOUP BOWL
*The Magical Negro Reveals His Secret* by Gabriel Green

2018 SUMMER TIDE POOL
*Yell* by Sarah Sousa

2018 WINTER SOUP BOWL
*Paleotemptestology* by Bertha Crombet

*White Boys from Hell* by Jeffrey Skinner

2017 SUMMER TIDE POOL
*Atypical Cells of Undetermined Significance* by Brenna Womer

2017 WINTER SOUP BOWL
*Heredity and Other Inventions* by Sharona Muir

*On Inaccuracy* by Joe Manning

2016 SUMMER TIDE POOL
*Cuntstruck* by Kate Northrop

*Relief Map* by Erin M. Bertram

*Love Undefined* by Jonathan Katz

2016 WINTER SOUP BOWL
*Notes from the Negro Side of the Moon* by Earl Braggs

*A Hunger Called Music: A Verse History in Black Music*
by Meredith Nnoka

www.ingramcontent.com/pod-product-compliance
Lightning Source LLC
Chambersburg PA
CBHW030814090426
42737CB00010B/1267